A N

Dorling K
new progr
conjunctio
Cliff Moon M.Ed., Honorary
of Reading.

Beautiful illustrations and superb full-colour photographs combine with engaging, easy-to-read stories to offer a fresh approach to each subject in the series. Each *Dorling Kindersley Classic Reader* is guaranteed to capture a child's interest while developing his or her reading skills, general knowledge and love of reading.

The four levels of *Dorling Kindersley Classic Readers* are aimed at different reading abilities, enabling you to choose the books that are exactly right for your children.

Level One – Beginning to read
Level Two – Beginning to read alone
Level Three – Reading alone
Level Four – Proficient readers

The "normal" age at which a child begins to read can be anywhere from three to eight years old, so these levels are intended only as a general guideline.

No matter which level you select, you can be sure that you are helping your child learn to read, then read to learn!

www.dk.com

Created by Leapfrog Press Ltd

Project Editor Caryn Jenner
Art Editor Paul Effeny

For Dorling Kindersley
Senior Editor Marie Greenwood
Managing Art Editor Jacquie Gulliver
Managing Editor Joanna Devereux
Production Chris Avgherinos
Picture Researcher Liz Moore
Cover Design Margherita Gianni

Reading Consultant
Cliff Moon M.Ed.

Published in Great Britain by
Dorling Kindersley Ltd
9 Henrietta Street
London WC2E 8PS

2 4 6 8 10 9 7 5 3 1

Dorling Kindersley Classic Readers™ is a trademark
of Dorling Kindersley Ltd, London.

Text copyright © 2000 Rosalind Kerven
Illustration and compilation copyright © 2000
Dorling Kindersley Ltd.

A CIP catalogue record for this book is available
from the British Library.

ISBN 0-7513-6725-7

Colour reproduction by Colourscan, Singapore
Printed and bound in Belgium by Proost

Key = a = above, b = below, l = left, r = right, c = centre

The publisher would like to thank the following:
Bridgeman Art Library: 46b; Mary Evans Picture Library: 18b, 25t;
Kobal Collection: 4; Sothebys: 5; Tony Stone Images: 30.

Additional photography by: Chester Betty, British Museum

Contents

CLASSIC READERS

READING
3
ALONE

ALADDIN

AND OTHER TALES FROM
THE ARABIAN NIGHTS

Retold by Rosalind Kerven

Illustrated by
Nilesh Mistry

DK
www.dk.com
London • New York • Sydney • Auckland • Delhi

Arabian Nights

A thousand years ago, the Arabian Empire stretched across North Africa, through the Middle East, all the way to India.

Many of its people spoke Arabic and followed the Muslim religion. They told wonderful tales of magic and adventure.

One of these tales was about Queen Shahrazad (sh-hara-zard). Her husband, the king, planned to kill her. But every night, Shahrazad told him a story.

Shahrazad

The king allowed Shahrazad to live so she could finish telling her stories. He ended up falling in love with her.

The king thought these stories were wonderful. He spared her life so that he could hear more of them.

The stories were finally collected and called *The Arabian Nights*.

You can read some of the most exciting ones in this book.

Aladdin and the Lamp

Once there was an evil magician who longed to have all the treasure in the world.

One night, the magician chanted a strange spell. As the flames and coloured mist rose up, he saw the picture of a dark cave. A magic lamp lay hidden deep inside it.

This lamp had power over many treasures. But only one person could enter the cave to get it. This was a boy who lived far away in China. His name was Aladdin. The magician flew across the world to meet him.

At last, among the silks and spices in
a market, the magician heard a voice
calling, "Aladdin, you trouble-maker!"

A young boy laughed as he raced
between the market stalls.

The evil magician grabbed Aladdin
and quickly dragged him away.

The magician took Aladdin far
away to a lonely mountain and made
another spell of fire and incense.
There was a clap of
thunder and the ground
shook beneath them.

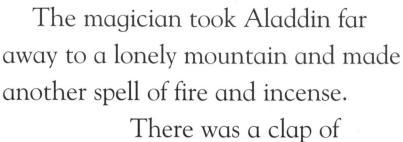

As Aladdin watched, a hole appeared
in the mountain. In the hole was a stone
slab with a gleaming brass ring.

"Go down and bring me the lamp
from the Enchanted Garden," ordered
the magician. "Take this with you."
He slipped a ring onto Aladdin's finger.

The magician pushed the boy towards
the slab. It opened like a door and
Aladdin suddenly found himself in an
enormous cave. His heart pounded.

Fragrant incense
Burning incense makes a
sweet-smelling smoke.
This incense burner is
made of silver and gold.

*Incense
burner*

Incense

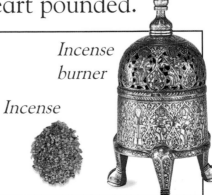

Aladdin walked through the cave into an Enchanted Garden. The trees were full of fruit. But when Aladdin looked closely, he saw that the fruits were actually sparkling glass marbles. He stuffed some into his pockets, then hurried on.

At last, he saw an old brass oil lamp. Whatever did the magician want it for? Aladdin wrapped it inside his shirt for safety, then went back outside.

The magician was waiting for him. "Hand it over," he snapped, trying to snatch the lamp from Aladdin.

Magic lamp
Oil lamps were common household objects. To Aladdin, the lamp in the cave looks quite ordinary.

But the lamp was caught
inside his shirt. The magician
gave Aladdin a hard slap. The force of it
made the boy fall right back into the cave
with the lamp. The stone slab slammed
tightly shut behind him.

The magician cursed and screamed
with rage. Then he flew away, back
across the world to hide.

Inside the cave, Aladdin panicked.
He was trapped! Was God punishing
him for being lazy and cheeky? What if
he had to stay in the cave forever?
Aladdin promised to live a useful life
if he escaped. He twisted his hands
together in despair and by mistake he
rubbed the magician's ring.

Suddenly, blue smoke spilled out of
the ring! The smoke took the shape
of a frightening genie.

"Master," the genie bellowed, "your
wish is my command."

At first, Aladdin was so surprised,
he could not speak. The genie waited.

"I wish I was at home," said Aladdin.

Almost before the words were out of his mouth, he was caught up in a dazzling whirlwind of coloured light. Round and round he spun, on and on through time and space.

Then everything grew still. Aladdin opened his eyes. He was safely back in his home. His mother stared at him in surprise. Breathlessly, he told her what had happened.

"Why can't you do something useful?" Aladdin's mother cried. "We have no money and no food."

Aladdin looked at the lamp from the cave. "I could sell that old lamp at the market," he offered.

"Who will buy that filthy old thing?" said his mother. "Here, let me polish it."

She rubbed her rag over the lamp. Suddenly there was a cloud of purple smoke and out sprung another, even bigger genie.

"What is your wish?" he bellowed.

"We wish for food and plenty of it!" cried Aladdin.

At once, a huge silver tray appeared,  full of food. Aladdin and his mother ate until they felt ready to burst. Then Aladdin remembered something.

"Look what I found in the Enchanted Garden," he said, showing his mother the coloured marbles.

Aladdin's mother gasped. She held the marbles up to the sun, so that a rainbow light danced out of them.

"Oh Aladdin!" she exclaimed. "These are not marbles. They are jewels! We are rich beyond our wildest dreams."

From that moment, life changed for Aladdin and his mother. They sold enough jewels to buy a grand house full of fine things and with many servants. They wore clothes made from rich silks. Thanks to the genie of the lamp, they dined on the most delicious food.

The years passed quickly. Aladdin grew into a handsome, bold young man.

One day Aladdin saw the princess, Badr al-Budur (Bah-der al-Bu-der) and fell in love with her at once. He asked the emperor if he could marry her. The emperor was impressed by Aladdin's extraordinary wealth. He agreed and a wonderful wedding feast was held. Afterwards, Aladdin commanded the genie of the lamp to conjure up a magnificent palace for them to live in.

But Aladdin never forgot his promise in the cave and often helped the poor people of the city. Everyone admired him. Things worked out very well for Aladdin.

But meanwhile, the evil magician was plotting his revenge.

One day, when Aladdin was away, the magician came to his palace disguised as a pedlar. He shouted: "Give me your old lamps and I'll give you new ones!"

When Princess Badr al-Budur heard him, she remembered the old lamp that Aladdin kept locked in a box. She told her servant to give it to the pedlar.

The magician snatched the lamp and ran to a dark corner. As he rubbed it, the genie appeared in purple smoke.

Pedlars

Pedlars travelled around towns and villages selling or exchanging goods.

"What is your wish?" the genie asked.

"Bring Aladdin's palace and all his riches to my own land," hissed the magician. "And bring the princess, too."

In a flash of light the genie obeyed, and the magician's wish came true.

So the princess and the palace disappeared. The emperor blamed Aladdin. He ordered his guards to arrest Aladdin when he returned to the city.

"Your fancy palace was a conjuring trick," the emperor raged. "Now it has vanished – and so has my daughter!"

Aladdin knew that this was the work of the evil magician, but the emperor would not listen. Instead, he locked Aladdin up in prison.

The people of the city
wanted to free Aladdin,
but the emperor said that
he must die.

Luckily, Aladdin
remembered the magician's
magic ring. He felt for it
on his finger and rubbed it.
At once the genie appeared.

"What is your wish?" he bellowed.

"I want my palace back," Aladdin
cried. "And above all, I want my wife."

The genie shook his head. "I am
sorry. Your palace and your wife have
been stolen by the genie of the lamp.
His magic is stronger than mine so I
cannot grant your wish."

"Then take me to the palace,
wherever it may be," said Aladdin.

In a flash, Aladdin found himself with his princess in their palace. "The evil magician wants to marry me," she sobbed. "He bullies me when I refuse."

Aladdin made a plan. He told the genie of the ring to bring sleeping herbs.

That night, the princess dressed in her finest robes. She gave the magician a cup of wine. He did not know that Aladdin had put sleeping herbs in it! The magician fell into a deep sleep.

Silver cup

The princess may have served wine in a Chinese silver drinking cup similar to this one.

Aladdin snatched the magic lamp. Then he told the mighty genie of the lamp to move everything back to China.

The emperor apologized to Aladdin and banished the evil magician. Many years went by. At last the old emperor died. Aladdin became the new emperor and ruled in happiness and peace.

The Garden of Enchantments

There was once a king who walked around in disguise to see what his people were doing.

One day, he heard three sisters talking. The first said, "I wish I could marry the king's pastrycook so I can feast on pastries."

The second said, "I want to marry the king's chef and have delicious dinners."

Then the third voice whispered, "My sisters, I wish to marry the king!"

The king made all the girls' wishes come true. But the older girls soon grew jealous when their younger sister became the new queen.

When the queen had a baby, her sisters stole it and put a dead puppy in its place. They changed her next two babies for a dead kitten and a dead mouse. The king was shocked and locked the queen away.

The wicked sisters had put the babies in baskets and floated them on the river. They were rescued by the king's gardener. He called the eldest boy Farid, the second boy Faruz and the girl Farizad.

Time passed happily. Then the gardener and his wife died, leaving their house and beautiful garden to the children.

One day, Farizad was
at home alone when an
old woman knocked
upon the gate.
Farizad led her into
the garden. The old
woman looked
around her.

"My dear," she said,
"you may believe that this
garden is beautiful but it is missing three
things: the Talking Bird, the Singing
Tree and the Golden Water. Until you
bring them here you can never be happy."

"How can I find them?" asked Farizad.

The old woman looked into her eyes.

"You must travel towards India for
twenty days. Then you will meet a man
who will tell you all you need to know."

Farizad told her brothers about the Talking Bird, the Singing Tree and the pure Golden Water. Farid said, "I'm the eldest, so I will search for them." He gave his knife to Farizad. "As long as this blade is clean, you will know I am safe."

He set off on his journey and for twenty days all was well.

Persian armour
Farizad sets off to find her brothers disguised as a warrior for protection. This Persian warrior's helmet is partly made of chainmail.

But the next day, Farid's
knife turned rusty.

Faruz gave Farizad
a necklace. "I must
go after Farid.
While these
pearls glow,
I am safe."

But on the twenty-first morning, the
pearls turned dry as bones. Farizad rode
swiftly out to help her brothers.

After twenty days, Farizad met a holy man. "Have you seen my brothers?" she asked him. "They are searching for the Talking Bird, the Singing Tree and the Golden Water."

The holy man nodded sadly, "I tried to help them but they forgot my advice and got into trouble." He gave Farizad a red rock. "Roll this up the mountain. If you reach the top, all will be well. But do not listen to the voices you hear on the way or you will turn to stone!"

Farizad rolled the rock up the mountain. Soon voices called to her:

"Help! Help! Please save us, sister Farizad!"

Bravely, she ignored them and climbed higher up the mountain. At last the voices faded. She had reached the top!

31

At the top of the mountain, the Talking Bird was waiting. The Singing Tree played a beautiful tune and the Golden Water sparkled like gold.

"Oh Bird," cried Farizad, "all this is wonderful. But where are my brothers?"

"I will help you," said the Bird. "But first pick a branch of the Singing Tree to take back to your garden," the Bird told her. "Then fill this jar with Golden Water. I will lead you home. On the way, you must sprinkle some Water over every rock we pass."

Farizad followed the Bird down the mountain, sprinkling Golden Water on the rocks. Each one turned into a young man and two of them were Farid and Faruz! Farizad hugged them joyfully. Then together they travelled home.

The Talking Bird built a nest in the garden. The branch grew into a new Singing Tree. The Golden Water sparkled like sunshine in the fountain. It was truly a garden of enchantments!

One day, the king came to see the
garden. Farizad cooked stuffed
cucumbers for him and the Bird
told her to fill them with pearls.
The king nearly choked.
"Who has heard of cucumbers
stuffed with pearls?" he cried.

"Who has heard of a queen
giving birth to a puppy, a
kitten or a mouse?" replied the
Bird. It flew to Farid. "Here is
your puppy." Off it flew to
Faruz. "This is your kitten."

34

Lastly, it flew to Farizad. "And this is your mouse! Their wicked aunts almost killed your babies. But luckily they were rescued."

Indeed, now the king could see by their faces that they were his children. How foolish and cruel he had been.

Together, they went to find the queen. She was overjoyed to see her children and forgave the king. And they all lived happily ever after.

Ali Baba and the Forty Thieves

Something strange was happening in the forest. Forty nasty-looking men carried sacks of gold to a large rock. Their chief cried, "OPEN, SESAME!" and the rock opened like a door.

They all trooped inside. The rock shut fast behind them. Minutes passed. Then there came a muffled cry of "OPEN, SESAME!" Out came the robbers dragging empty sacks. The rock closed and they rode away.

Ali Baba was watching in a tree. He was astonished by what he saw and heard. He climbed down and crept up to the rock, then whispered the robber's words, "Open, sesame!"

Sesame

Sesame was one of many crops grown by Arabian farmers. The tasty seeds can be used in cooking, raw or toasted.

The rock
slid open. Ali Baba
stepped in and the rock
closed behind him. He crept
through the darkness into a
great cave. Ali Baba gasped. The cave
was full of sparkling treasure!

"I'm not a greedy man," he thought.
"God must want me to be rich."

Quickly, he grabbed two sacks of gold.
Then he said the magic words, sneaked
out and hurried home.

"Look at the treasure I've brought you!" he called to his wife.

At first, she was suspicious. But by the time he had finished his story, his wife was jumping with excitement.

"We must keep this a secret," Ali Baba warned her. "Let's dig a hole and hide the treasure inside."

"You dig," she said. "I'll borrow a scoop from your brother, Kasim. Then we'll measure how much gold we have."

Before Ali Baba could stop her, she rushed next door.

Allah's will
Ali Baba follows the Muslim religion.
He believes that he was guided to the treasure by Allah (God), so that he can be rich.

Ali Baba's wife would not tell Kasim why she wanted the scoop. Kasim's wife was suspicious, so she smeared a little sticky suet on the bottom of the scoop, then handed it over. Soon Ali Baba's wife brought back the scoop, not realizing that a gold coin was stuck to it.

"Kasim," cried his wife, "your brother has a pile of gold. Make him share it with us!"

So Ali Baba was forced to tell his brother about the robbers' cave. Kasim hurried off to get some gold.

"OPEN, SESAME!" The rock opened and Kasim went into the cave.

He gathered
up as much treasure as he
could, then turned back to the rock.

"OPEN…" What was the other
word? "OPEN, OATS? OPEN, RICE?"

Just then, the forty robbers returned.
When they found Kasim in the cave,
they chopped him into little pieces.

The robbers were furious that Ali Baba's family knew about their secret hide-out.

Their chief disguised himself as an olive oil merchant and went to Ali Baba's house with forty huge clay jars.

He pretended to need a place to stay. "Do stay with us," Ali Baba offered. He did not recognize the robber chief!

Ali Baba's servants unloaded the heavy jars. But only one jar really contained oil. The others contained the evil robbers, hiding while they waited for the signal to kill Ali Baba.

Late that night, a servant girl called Marjana went to the jars to fetch some oil for her lamp. But when she dipped her cup into a jar, it bumped against one of the robber's heads!

Olive oil

Black olives are pressed to make olive oil, which can be used for lighting lamps. Olive oil is still used in cooking today.

Marjana quickly guessed what the robbers were planning to do. She boiled a big pot of oil, then poured the hot liquid onto the wicked men's heads.

Soon the chief found his robbers boiled to a frazzle. Then he saw Marjana and realized that she was to blame. How could she escape him? Quickly, she put on a beautiful costume. As she danced, she flashed a golden dagger to and fro. The chief leapt up to grab it. As they struggled, Marjana thrust the dagger straight into his heart.

Daggers
Arabian dancers like Marjana often waved daggers as they danced. The daggers were not meant to be used as weapons.

"You have
saved my life!" cried
Ali Baba. He took
Marjana to the secret cave.
"OPEN, SESAME!" he cried for the last
time. Marjana took enough treasure to
live like a queen for the rest of her days.

Arabian Days

The stories in *The Arabian Nights* contain magic, but they are firmly rooted in the daily life of the Arabian Empire.

The stories were told aloud in market-places in the heart of Islamic towns. On narrow streets crammed with stalls, passers-by stopped to browse and chat. Storytellers competed for attention with pedlars and merchants. Their stories told of ordinary characters, such as tradesmen, woodcutters and slaves, as well as kings and beautiful princesses.

Business travel

Arab merchants heard stories in the market-places. When they went abroad to trade, they spread the stories far and wide.

In Arabian society, women were not equal to men but could own property and were often educated. Farizad and Marjana are shown as strong, resourceful women in the stories.

The great Arab Empire eventually divided into separate countries. But its rich culture lives on through its stories.

Glossary

Allah
The Muslim name for God.

Arabian
Belonging to the Arabic-speaking peoples of the Middle East and North Africa.

Astonished
To be almost unable to believe that something has happened.

Despair
Giving up hope that things will go right.

Disguised
Dressed up in a costume to look like someone or something else.

Enchanted
A place or thing that is so delightful that it feels as though something magical has happened to it.

Empire
A group of countries that are under the control of a ruler, called an emperor.

Genie
A genie often comes from an object, such as a lamp or a ring, and can only carry out the wishes of the person who owns the object.

Incense
Herbs or spices that are ground up and burned to make a sweet smell.

Islam
The Muslim religion, which was founded by the prophet, Muhammad.

Merchant
A person who buys and sells goods for money.

Persia
(per-sha)
The old name for the country of Iran, in the Middle East. Baghdad (bag-dad) was the capital of Persia.

Potion
(po-shun)
A magic drink.

Resourceful
Sensible and clever. Able to deal with difficult situations.

Suet
Animal fat used in cooking and for making soap and candles.

Suspicious
(su-spish-us)
Thinking that something wrong or bad is happening.